Silence and Lost Words

POEMS

Rouhangiz Karachi

SELECTED AND TRANSLATED BY

Mojdeh Bahar

BILINGUAL EDITION

MAGE PUBLISHERS

Mage Publishers Inc
www.mage.com

Library of Congress Cataloging-in-Publication Data
Available at the Library of Congress

Bilingual hardcover edition
ISBN 978-1-949445-85-5

Email: as@mage.com ·
Mage online: www.mage.com

To my brother Reza

Contents

Translator's Preface

Studying and translating the works of over one hundred contemporary Persian women poets, I have admired the diversity among these poets' voices, tropes, styles, and lexicon. Their masterful use of language, sometimes veiled and suggestive, other times direct and assertive, is complex and nuanced. Though I find translation to be an immersive process, some poems take flight after the translation and revisions have been completed. There is a definitive ending to their journey from one language to another. Other poems linger—they turn round and round in my head, and have me play with an endless number of words. Conveying their essence is complex and all-consuming. They are never fully translated for I always fear that there may be a better way to capture them.

Rouhangiz Karachi's poems have haunted me. I find them to be deeply sorrowful. The images are dark and impactful. They depict women's social struggles and internal tensions. For over forty years, Karachi's scholarly work has also focused on Iranian women, poets and protagonists alike. Karachi's "woman" appears universal. Very few of her poems have a uniquely regional or ethnic color, allowing all readers to identify with her poems. and be deeply affected by them.

The poet describes her first collection of poems, *Ān Ruz-ha ke Shahrnaz Budam* (Back when I was Shahrnaz), as "romantic and sad." The second collection, *Kābus-ha-ye Zan* (Woman's nightmares) is marked by struggles, movements and the complicated relationship between the poet and words. The third collection, *Cheshm-ha-ye Luch-e Zamin* (Earth's crossed eyes) focuses on the tension between a weary world and the wandering poet. The fourth collection, *Sokut-e In Suy-e Khat-ha-ye Dar Ham* (Silence on this side of the jumbled lines) vacillates between a quest for hope, for a better future; and the poet's resignation to a lonely existence. The unpublished poems seem to grow more anxious. They reflect a particular angst concerned with words, paper, poetry and the process of writing.

In autumn of 2018, Karachi published a selection of her poetry, chronologically arranging her poems from each of the four collections. Perusing the selection, the reader readily appreciates Karachi's poetic journey through the years.

In this bilingual collection of her work, I have used her 2018 collection in Persian, but have further narrowed down the selections and included eleven of her unpublished poems. I have adhered to grouping poems from the same collection together, hoping the reader will have a similar experience to mine. I have endeavored to select poems that have more universal themes. I have also tried to preserve the voice of the poet by translating the poet's introductory texts and comments in a preface. I have taken the liberty of introducing each of the references in the introductory texts and adding explanatory notes where necessary for a more seamless reading experience. Where comprehension of the text was not compromised, I have adopted the poet's neologisms of patient-land, sorrow-land, and such in the English translations.

In taking a deeper dive in the poetry of Rouhangiz Karachi and surrendering to their profound impact I am convinced that the Iranian love affair with Persian poetry for at least the past 1,000 years is something we need to preserve and to pass on so we can continue to read poems and take note of poets on a more routine basis in our daily lives.

Maryland, October 2024

در گور زاده شدم

به روایت مادرم فرنگیس که موثق‌ترین راوی بود،
چهارده روز پیش از عید نوروز ۱۳۳۳ گریه‌کنان آمده
بودم. در شهری که سرسختی اساطیری‌اش را نام‌های
چهارگانه‌اش افشا می‌کنند. اردشیر خره، گور، جور،
فیروزآباد. مسعودی در مروج الذهب آن را با خاک
خوب و هوای صاف از گردشگاه‌های فارس می‌داند.
ابن‌حوقل گردشگاه‌ها و باغ‌ها و قصرها و مناظر عالی و
دلربا و فرح‌بخش و سبز و خرم آن را می‌ستاید. جیهانی
آن را شهری به‌غایت خوش توصیف می‌کند. مقدسی
گور را شهری خوش و زیبا و دلگشا و فرحزا و مرکز
گل می‌داند. اردشیر بابکان کاخش را آنجا بنا می‌کند
و پایتختش را آنجا می‌نهد. عضدالدوله گردشگاه و
شکارگاهش را فیروزآباد نام‌گذاری می‌کند، من... امّا
جز دیوار وُ فقر ندیدم وَ انسان‌هایی که به هیچ قانع‌اند وُ
به هرچیز خود را نمی‌فروشند.

Poet's Preface

I Was Born in Gur

According to my mother, Farangis, the most reliable narrator, fourteen days before Nowruz of 1954, I entered this world, crying. In a city whose four names attest to its mythical persistence: Ardeshir Korra's splendor, Gur, Jur, and Firuzabad. With its fertile soil and pleasant climate, Massoudi, [tenth-century Arab historian and traveler], describes it as one of the attractions of Fars province. Ibn Howqal, [tenth-century Arab geographer and traveler], praises its attractions, gardens, castles; green, lush and beautiful vistas. Jayhāni, [Persian vizier of the Samanid Empire], describes it as a beautiful city. Moqadassi, [medieval Arab geographer], classifies Gur as a beautiful and exhilarating city, a center for flowers. Ardeshir Babakan, [the founder of Sasanid Empire in the third century], built his castle there and made the city his capital. Azeddodoleh named his place of leisure and hunting, Firuzabad. I, however, observed nothing but walls and poverty. I saw people who were satisfied with very little to nothing and would not readily sell themselves.

از آن روزهای دور که مادر با قصه‌های اسکندر و یوسف مرا به سرزمینِ گستردهٔ ادبیات برد تنها خاطره‌ای کمرنگ به‌جا مانده و نشانه‌هایی از سخت‌کوشی اسکندر و بی‌اعتمادی یوسف در من... امّا فضای قدیمی یادم سرشار غزل‌های حافظ است و لحن خواندن مادربزرگ... صدای برادر با قصه‌های هدایت... دست‌های زبر پدر و خستهٔ مادر.

[...]

مادر زنی با استعداد و با فرهنگ بود و پدر مردی خودساخته و باهوش، که در آن شهر محروم برای باسواد کردن چهار فرزند رنج‌های بسیاری را به جان خریدند. برادر بزرگم معلم ادبیات است و سال‌ها برای کاغذهایش داستان می‌نویسد. خواهرم معلم است و استعداد نقاشی‌اش را فدای روزمَرگی زندگی می‌کند. برادر کوچک‌ترم تحصیلات سینمایی دارد و فیلمساز و فیلمنامه‌نویس است. همسرم استاد زیست‌شناسی است و دخترم سپند دکترای تنوع زیستی و پسرم سهند دکترای معماری می‌خواند. خودم عطش خواندن دارم.

این روزها سرگشته‌تر از دردم...، نابسامانی‌های پیرامونم، جنگ، ویرانی، دروغ، دزدی، خیانت، فساد، گرسنگی و فقر و آوارگی نسل جوان چنان بی‌تابم می‌کند که به شعر پناه می‌برم تا در جهان پر راز و رمزش گم شوم.

شعر برایم همیشه پناهگاه ایمنی بوده است و نجات دهنده‌ای بِخرد. نخستین معجزه شعر برایم روزی بود که خواندن دوسه بیت شعر نظامی، در شش‌سالگی مجوز ورودم به دبستان شد. بعدها در دورهٔ دبیرستان

Of those long-gone days when mom would transport me to the vast literary lands with stories of Alexander and Joseph, only pale memories, signs of Alexander's diligence and Joseph's suspicion, have stayed with me. But my old recollections are filled with Hafez's ghazals and my grandmother's voice... my brother's reading of Hedayat's stories... father's rough and mother's weary hands.

[...]

Mom was a cultured and talented woman. Dad was an intelligent, self-made man. In that underserved city they suffered a great deal to educate their four children. My eldest brother is a literature teacher who writes stories. My sister is a teacher who has sacrificed her artistic talent in painting to earn a living. My younger brother studied film and is a screenwriter and director. My husband is a biology professor. My daughter Sepand has her Ph.D. in biodiversity and my son Sahand has his Ph.D. in architecture. As for me, I have a thirst for reading.

These days I am bewildered by pain, the chaos around me, war, destruction, lies, theft, betrayal, corruption, hunger, poverty, and displacement of the younger generation. They make me so agitated that I seek refuge in poetry, lose myself in its mysterious world.

Poetry has always been a safe haven, a learned savior for me. The first miracle of poetry occurred for me when I recited three lines of a poem by Nezami [the medieval romantic epic poet]. It became my ticket to enter primary school one year early, at the age of six. Later, during my high school

فرمول‌های شیمی با دوبیتی در حافظه‌ام بیشتر می‌ماند و شعر ابزاری شد که نمره‌های بهتری بگیرم در درس‌های اجباری. اکنون جهانِ شعر، زندگی را برایم قابل تحمل‌تر می‌کند و تلخی‌های جهان را با شعر تاب می‌آورم.

تهران، دوم دی‌ماه ۱۳۹۶

پرسش: چرا شعر می‌گویید؟

شعر

۱۳۴۶ سال‌های شورشِ احساس بود وُ طوفانِ فریادی در من می‌خروشید که راهی به بیرون نمی‌جُست. کلیدِ دهانم در دستِ اطرافیانی مسلّط و مردم سنتیِ شهری بود که در صندوقچه‌ی باورِ خویش مراقبش بودند. جوش وُ خروشِ احساس وُ نیازی درونی در چهاردیواریِ خانه‌ی «چراغعلی‌خان» با هراس بر کاغذ نقش بست و بعدها، خانِ کوچکِ خانه‌ی ما، برادرم «عبدالحسین‌خان» که او هم برای «سایه‌اش» داستان می‌نوشت، مُهر تأیید و نشر آن‌ها را البته با شرط، تصویب کرد و من با نام ساختگی «شهرناز» شاعرِ ناشناسِ دیار انزوا شدم (۱۳۵۰).

years, rhyming enabled me to remember chemical formulas better, and thus poetry became a helpful tool in improving my grades in required courses. Nowadays, the world of poetry makes life more tolerable for me and with it I can better withstand the world's hardships.

Tehran, December 23, 2017

[The editors of certain anthologists would send questions to their writers. What appears below is the poet's response to one such question, namely: Why do you write poetry?]

Poetry[2]

1967 was the year feelings revolted. A storm of outcries was gathering within me, finding no outlet. The key to my mouth was held by dominant family members and traditional people who guarded it in their safe of beliefs. Within the confines of Cheragh Ali khan's house, tumultuous feelings and an internal need fearfully took shape on paper. Later, my youngest brother, Abdul Hossein khan, who also wrote stories, conditionally approved their publication under the pseudonym of "Shahrnaz," and I became the unknown poet of the land of isolation (1972).

بازتاب جهانِ درونی‌ام کاغذهای زیادی را سیاه کرد و دریافتم جوششِ احساس، بی‌خروشِ اندیشه، پیچیدگیِ ذهن مرا تصویر نمی‌کند. سال‌هاست سرگشته در گستره‌ی شعر می‌دوم و بی‌هراس در جست‌وجوی آن راهم. دیگر از تهدیدهای همسرم که دفترهای شعرم را پاره کند نمی‌لرزم، که آن را محصول ذهنیت مردانه در جامعه‌ای مرد برتر می‌دانم و از تحقیرهای برادر کوچک‌تر و پسرم نیز دلخور نیستم. از آن هم بیم ندارم که چرا مردانِ شاعر جدی‌ام نگرفتند. دلشده‌ی آفریدنم و سال‌هاست در دشت‌های اندیشه سرگردان...

تهران، ۱۳۷۵[1]

شعر زنانه

این روزها که گذر سی ساله‌ی کاری‌ام را با سفارش می‌نویسم، اعتراف می‌کنم که پژوهش‌های اجباری هم مرا از دغدغه‌ی نوشتن درباره‌ی زنان شاعر دور نکرده، درست از سال ۱۳۶۰ که پایان‌نامه‌ام را با موضوعِ شعر زنانه و زنان شاعر در میانه‌ی دو انقلاب نوشتم تاکنون سعی کرده‌ام در تقابل با نگاه مردانه‌ای که در طول تاریخ، چهره‌ی تحریف‌شده‌ای از زنانِ هنرمند ساخته، آن‌ها را نادیده گرفته و به حاشیه رانده و فرصت نوشتن و سرودن را از آن‌ها گرفته هزاران صفحه کاغذ را سیاه کنم و به رویکرد مردانه‌ی حاکم در ادبیات و آن هنجارِ مردنوشت و سنت ادبی تک‌جنسیتی که چهره‌ای ناشایست از زنِ شاعر ارائه داده اعتراض کنم و به جبران این غفلت

The expression of my internal world filled many pages and I learned that tumultuous feelings, without rigorous thought, fail to describe the complexity of my mind. For many years, I have been wandering in the vast landscape of poetry and I am fearless in charting my path. I no longer shudder at my spouse's threats to tear my poetry notebooks to pieces, as I perceive it to be the result of the masculine mindset in a patriarchal society. Nor am I upset by my little brother and my son's insults. I no longer fear being dismissed by male poets. I am passionate about creating, and for years I have been wandering in the fields of thought...

Tehran, 1996

FEMININE POETRY

As I write about my thirty-year career, I admit that even required research projects have not distracted me from working on women poets. Since 1982—when I wrote my dissertation on feminine poetry and the poetry of women between the Constitutional and Islamic revolutions—when encountering the male perspective responsible for the inaccurate depiction of women artists, their marginalization, their being denied the opportunity to write and compose throughout history; I have written thousands of pages objecting to the dominant male approach, male/masculine writing, and the single-gender literary tradition that paints an unbecoming picture of women poets. In order

تاریخی ارزش سروده‌های مغلوب و فراموش‌شده‌ی زنان را بازنمایی کنم و پاسخی علمی به پرسش مردان روزگار خود دهم که چرا شعر را به زنانه و مردانه تقسیم کرده‌ام.

با بررسی شعر زنانه و مردانه فارسی و با توجه به دیدگاه دانشمندان علوم زیستی، جامعه‌شناسی، روان‌شناسی، زبان‌شناسی و ادبیات متوجه تفاوت‌هایی شدم که جنسیت به‌عنوان متغیر همراه با مجموعه‌ای از این عوامل بر ذهن، رفتار، نگاه، تجربه، زبان و نوشتار تأثیرگذار است. شعر زنان به‌لحاظ فضای ذهنی، درون‌مایه، زمینه‌ی فکر و ویژگی‌های زبانی، آهنگ کلام و لحن بیان، واژگان، کاربرد صور خیال مانند استعاره و تشبیه، مضامین عاطفی و حسی و نوع بیانِ احساسی عاطفی و حتی ژانر شعری در شعر کلاسیک فارسی با شعر مردانِ شاعر تفاوت دارد.

در مطالعه‌ی شعرشناسی جنسیت پی بردم که در طول تاریخ شعر فارسی، نخستین شعرهای زنانه که جهانِ ذهنی بی‌نقاب زنانه را بیان می‌کند در قالب لالایی‌ها و سوگ‌سروده‌های شفاهی بوده است درحالی که برای مردان، با گذر از دوره‌ی اشعار چوپانی، شعر از همان آغاز ابزار کسب درآمد و دریافت صله بوده، به‌علاوه تأثیر جنس و جنسیت بر گزینش نوع یا ژانر شعری تأثیرگذار بوده و زنان شاعر بیشتر شعر غنایی سروده‌اند تا شعر حماسی و عرفانی و تعلیمی، چون ساختار ذهنی در شعر غنایی بیان احساسات درونی، عاطفی و آرزوهای یک شاعر است که آن را برای خود سروده است اما شعر حماسی و تعلیمی عینی و بیان جهانِ بیرونی است و شاعر با هدفِ خاصی آن را برای دیگران سروده است.

to make up for this historical neglect of poems by women, I want to revisit them and find a scientific answer to the men who ask why I have divided poems by gender.

In researching feminine and masculine Persian poetry, considering scholars of biology, sociology, psychology, linguistics, and literature, I noticed that gender as a variable along with other factors, affect mindset, behavior, vantage point, experience and language. Women's poetry and its intellectual framework, themes, thoughts, linguistic characteristics, musicality, tone, lexicon, and the use of literary devices such as metaphors and similes, sensual and sentimental topics, and the expression of feelings, even genre in classical persian poetry, differs from that of men.

In studying gendered poetics throughout the history of Persian poetry, I have learned that the first feminine poems, unveiling women's sentiments, were in the form of oral lullabies and elegies. For their male counterparts—after pastoral poetry— since its inception, poetry served as a way to earn a living or win a prize. In addition, the effect of gender on poetic genres is pronounced. Women wrote lyrical poetry as opposed to epic, spiritual, or didactic poetry because the lyrical genre was the expression of inner feelings and the hopes of a poet, written primarily for herself. Whereas epic or didactic poetry is the objective depiction of an outside world intended for others.

جامعه‌ی ادبی مردمحور ما، پیشینه‌ی ۱۰ قرن شعر زنانه و دوصدایی را نادیده گرفته و به‌عمد به فراموشی سپرده است. در طول این سال‌ها سعی کرده‌ام تصویری نزدیک به واقعیت از زنان شاعر آن‌چنان که در حاشیه‌ی جریان تاریخ ادبی ایران بوده‌اند در مقالات (که از حوصله‌ی این نوشته بیرون است) و کتاب‌هایی چون اندیشه‌نگاران زن در شعر مشروطه، عالم‌تاج قائم‌مقامی (ژاله)، پروین اعتصامی، فروغ فرخزاد، حیران دنبلی و در تاریخ شعر زنان از آغاز تا سده‌ی هشتم هجری ارائه دهم و از شعر زنانه و تجربه‌های آن‌ها بنویسم. حتی در تصحیح نسخه‌های خطی چون بانوگشسپ‌نامه، خشونت مشفقانه و هشت رساله در بیان احوال زنان هم دستنویس‌هایی با محوریت زن را در نظر داشتم تا موقعیت زنان را در ادبیات نوشتاری و در تاریخ اجتماعی ایران پیش روی خواننده بگذارم، باشد تا بازخوانی واقعیت‌های گذشته، رفتار ناشایست جامعه را نسبت به زنان تغییر دهد.

Our male-centric literary community has ignored ten centuries of women's poetry and intentionally obliviated the existence of two separate voices. For many years I have tried to depict an accurate image of women poets present on the margins of literary movements in articles (which is outside the scope of this text) and in books such as *Andisheh Negārān-e Zan dar She'r-e Mashruteh* (Women thought chroniclers in the poetry of the Constitutional Revolution), Ālamtāj Qāemmaqāmi (Zhāleh), Parvin Etessami, Forugh Farrokhzad, Heyrān Donboli, and in *Tārikh-e She'r-e Zanān az Āghāz tā Sadeh-ye Hashtom-e Hejri* (History of women's poetry from the beginning until the fifteenth century); and to speak of women's poetry and their experiences. Even in editing manuscripts of *"Bānu Goshasb Nameh"* (The book of lady goshasb), *"Khoshunat-e Moshfeqaneh"* (Benevolent aggression) and *Hasht Resāleh dar Bayan-e Ahvāl-e Zanān* (Eight essays on women's condition), I have been mindful in choosing women-centric themes to present women's position in the written tradition and social history of Iran to the reader. May rereading the past change the inappropriate treatment of women!

و... امّا معتقدم

در ادبیاتی که اندیشه و احساسِ انسانِ خردگرای ایرانی
در رباعیات خیام، غزل‌های حافظ و سعدی و مولانا
و مثنوی‌های فردوسی و نظامی و... و... به زیباترین
صورت ممکن به یادگار مانده است، نَه این نوشته‌ها
شعر است وُ نَه من شاعر. سیاهيِ این سطرها تجربه‌ی
زیسته‌ی زنی است در حوالی سال‌های ۱۳۴۹-۱۳۹۵.

کارنامه‌ی من

کارنامه‌ام سیاه سیاه است. دفترهای خط خطی،
سطرهای درهم و برهم و ریخته پاشیده از سال‌های
دورِ....

دورِ.....

دور.......

حوالی سال‌های ۱۳۴۷ که پرنده‌های گریخته از گلویم
را پناه دادند.

خیال‌ها... رؤیاها... شادی‌ها... تکرارها... مرگ‌ها... و
شعرها که نگذاشتتد زندگی کنم و سکوت... سکوت که
همه را به واژه بدل کرد...

And yet....I believe

In a literary tradition where the thought and feelings of a rationalist Iranian is reflected with utmost beauty in Khayyam's quatrains, the ghazals[3] of Hafez, Sa'di, Rumi and Masnavis[4] of Ferdowsi and Nezami, ...these writings are not considered poetry, nor am I considered a poet. These writings are the lived experiences of a woman who lived circa 1970-2016.

My Report Card

My report card is black, black. Scribbles in
   notebooks, jumbled lines, scattered here and
   there from many...
                  many
                     many years ago.
Circa 1973 when I sheltered escaped birds in my
   throat.
Ideas...dreams...joys...repetitions...deaths...and
   poems that did not let me be, and silence...
   silence that turned everything to words.

Rouhangiz Karachi's Poetry

FROM THE COLLECTION
BACK WHEN I WAS SHAHRNAZ
(1969-1978)

From volumes of hand-written notes, some unpublished, and some published in magazines such as *Javānān* (Youth) and...and... sorrowful poems of a young girl who wrote about love as well as political poems that would not have been published in those years, I have picked 7 poems and I am glad that I did not publish my romantic and protest poems at the time. I now present you with the poems of a young adult to be included in my report card.[5]

من، میهمان تازه‌واردِ شب‌های باورم

من را نگاه دار

من با سیاهی چشم تو خو گرفته‌ام

بهراسارت چشمانم

بازش نگاه دار

من قاب خالیم

من را نگاه دار

تهران، ۱۳۵۳/۵/۱۱

I'm the newly-arrived guest of faithful nights

Keep me around.

I have grown accustomed to your black eyes

To captivate my eyes

Keep them open.

I am an empty picture frame

Keep me around.

Tehran, 2 August 1974

لاشه‌ها می‌لولند
ذهن‌ها می‌پوسند
وَ زمان بوی تعفن دارد
زنی از عشق سخن می‌گوید
واژه‌ها در دهنش می‌گندند
شهر طاعون‌زده‌ای می‌پوسد
وَ زمان بوی تعفن دارد

تهران، ۱۳۵۴

Corpses swarm
Minds decay
And time has a foul odor
A woman speaks of love
The words rot in her mouth
A plague-ridden city decays
And time has a foul odor

Tehran, 1975

FROM THE COLLECTION
WITH THE WOMAN'S NIGHTMARES
(1978–1997)

پرنده روی شاخه‌ی خشک درخت می‌لرزید

وَ من به سال‌ها فکر می‌کردم...

فردا...

دوباره خورشید تکرار می‌شود

کلاغ‌ها همیشه سیه‌پوشند

و شب‌پره‌ها هنوز سرگردان

من می‌خواهم

درخت...من...پرنده وُ خورشید را

متوقف کنم!

ستاره وُ شب‌ها ملولم کرده اند

۱۳۵۹/۱۲/۱۷ ،پونا

The bird was shivering on the dry branch
And I was thinking of all the years...
Tomorrow...
Once again the sun repeats itself
The crows are always dressed in black
And the moths are still in a tizzy
I want
to stop
the tree...myself...the bird...the sun
The star and nights have given me the blues

Pune, India, 8 March 1981

چهل سرود سیاه
در شامگاه دیروز
آواز تلخ کلاغان بود
بر سیم خاردار تنم

تهران، اسفند ۱۳۷۲

Forty black anthems
Yesterday evening
Were the bitter song of crows
On the barbed-wires of my body

Tehran, March 1994

چشمانم بر کرانه‌ی زمین
زبانِ سرخم بر دار...
من روییدم
زرد و کهربایی

تهران، ؟

My eyes on the shores of the earth
My red tongue on the gallows
I have grown
Yellow and amber

Tehran, n.d.

دلت را...
ورق که می‌زنی
خونِ خاطرات جاری می‌شود
من غرق می‌شوم
تنها می‌مانی!

تهران، ۱۳۷۶/۱۰/۲۹

Your heart...
As you leaf through it
The blood of memories pours out
I drown....
You are left alone

Tehran, 19 January 1998

قلم که برمی‌دارم
جهان را طوفان می‌برد
هیچ‌کس نیست
دروازه‌ها را ببندد
تنم با چهار دروازه باز به دنیا وصل است
شمالش به کابوس...
جنوب به مرگ...
شرق به گورستان...
و غربش شب‌های بی‌انتهاست...
خاکستر می‌شوم
دهان که باز می‌کنم
تا کهکشان چقدر راه است...
با گردباد بی‌تاب...؟

تهران، ۱۳۷۳

16

As I pick up the pen
The world is swept away by a flood
There's no one
To close the gates
My body with four open gates is
    connected to the world
Nightmares to the north...
Death to the south...
Cemetery to the east...
Endless nights to the west...
I am reduced to ashes
As I open my mouth
How far is it to the galaxy...
With the restless tornado...?

Tehran, 1994

گندابه...
من...
پرنده نیز...
به هیچ‌جا نرسیدیم
گندابه
آینه‌ی شکسته‌ی تکرار
وَ من در آستانه‌ی رفتن
پایم بریده بود
پرنده نیز...

به هیچ‌جا نرسیدیم

فیروزآباد، ۱۳۵۸

18

Swamp...

    I....

        The bird as well

We didn't get anywhere

Swamp

The broken mirror of repetition

And me, about to leave

My leg was cut

The bird's as well...

We didn't get anywhere

Firuzabad, 1979

وَ ماه...
در انتظارِ انفجار
وُ شب...
در انتظارِ بی‌ستارگی
وَ شب...تمام شب
صدای خشک مرگ
عقوبت کدام بی‌هراس لحظه‌ای است...؟
در آستان هول
حجم فکرمن به دار
به برگ بی‌ترنم کتاب
خطوط معوجی نشان شاعریم
و شیشه‌های قرص خواب...رامشم
صبور باش
سوار باد گفت:

فیروزآباد، خرداد، ۱۳۶۱

And the moon...
Awaiting explosion
And the night...
Waiting to be starless
And night...the whole night
The harsh sound of death
Is the penance for which reckless moment...?
On the verge of panic
The entirety of my thoughts on the gallows
On the soundless pages of the book
Crooked lines attesting to my being a poet
And bottles of sleeping pills...my calm
Be patient!
Said the wind rider.

Firuzabad, June 1982

جهان برشانه‌هایم بود
در بی‌تاریخی زمانی تاریک
از چینِ باورم زمین می‌لرزید
نارِ استمطاربه جانم
در گرگ‌ومیش تاریخ‌ها
با فریادی خاموش
هفت جان داشتم وَ
تحملی گزاف
زن بودم

تهران، خرداد ۱۳۷۵

The weight of the world on my
shoulders[6]
In the dateless time of darkness
My belief shook the world.
Body ablaze[7]
In the twilight of histories
With a silent outcry
I had seven lives and
Endless endurance
I was a woman!

Tehran, June 1996

به منقار هفت پرنده آویزانم
از گاوِ گمشدگی

به کابوس های هراس
به هفت گردون
در هفت دوزخ
به هفت زمین وُ هفت سیاره‌ی سرگردان...
مرا نمی‌یابند
گُمشدگان هفت جهان...

تهران، ۱۳۷۳

24

I am suspended from the beak of seven birds
In a lost era

In terrifying nightmares
In seven celestial orbs
In seven hells
In seven earths and seven bewildered planets...
They don't find me
The lost ones of the seven worlds

Tehran, 1994

نَه مُردگان انتظارم را می‌کِشند...
نَه زندگان در انتظارم بودند...
نَه خاک ریشه‌ام را نواخت...
نَه آسمان شاخه‌ام را...
گمشده‌ای در صبرزار...
آویخته بر غبارها...
که دنیا مرا از من گرفته است.

تهران، خرداد ۱۳۷۵

Neither the dead await me....
Nor did the living wait for me...
Neither the soil caressed my roots...
Nor the sky my branches...
Lost in the patience-land...
Suspended from dust particles...
As the world has robbed me of myself.

Tehran, June 1996

تو کیستی...؟

پرسید: از خودش، زن با دهانِ بستهی تکرار

حسِ مؤنثی نمرده، در جست و جوی گُلی در خاکروبهها...؟

پُرسان وگُمشده در بین گورها، دنبال گور خویش...؟

نومیدی زنی...در خاطرات سرافکندگی با کودکانِ کور...؟

زن...در چهار پنجره بسته

پرسید از خودش

تاراجِ ناتمام

تو کیستی...؟

تهران، ۷۶/۴/۳

Who are you...?

Asked the woman of herself, with the closed
  mouth of repetition

A dying feminine feeling, searching for a
  flower in the dumpster...?

Inquiring and lost among tombs, looking for
  her own tomb...?

A woman's disappointment...in shameful
  memories of blind children...?

The woman...with all four windows closed

Asked herself

Unfinished plunder

Who are you...?

Tehran, 25 May 1997

29

بر خاطره‌ی مخدوشِ کاغذ

وَحاشیه‌ی زندگی...

دیرینه وُ سمج

خوابی پر از صدای خنجر وُ شمشیر دوستی

در انتهای تنهایی است...

آشفته وُ مشوش

کلاغ‌های همیشه سیه‌پوش

نوک می‌زنند

به غوغای زندگی

بیدار می‌شوم

سیاه‌تر از خواب

بر آبگینه‌ی کِدری مخدوش

هنگامه‌ای است

شمشیرهای دوستی

چکاچاک گُرزهاست

وَمی‌گریزم به حاشیه‌ی سپیدی کاغذ

از بیمِ زندگی...

تهران، ۷۶/۳/۵

On the distorted memory of the paper
And on the margins of life...
Persistent and chronic
A dream filled with sounds of dagger and the
    sword of friendship
Is at the end of loneliness...
Disheveled and anxious
The eternally black-cloaked crows
Peck at
The clamor of life
I wake up
To a darker world
In the opaque distorted mirror
There is chaos
Swords of friendship
Are the clash of clubs
And I escape to the margins of the white paper
Afraid of life...

Tehran, 26 May 1997

ابری از کلاغ‌ها

یادِ مرا

تاریک کرد...

دروازه‌ای به سمت سیاهی

وَ صدای سکوت

در مرز میانِ من و تنم...زوزه می‌کشید

به انزوای قطاری پناه بردم

بیگانه می گذشت.......از روی زندگی

و خاطرات زخمی در من پناه گرفتند سیاهی بی دریغی

همسفرم بود

وَ تو نبودی...!

تهران، ۱۳۷۶

A cloud of crows
Clouded
My memory...
A gate facing darkness
And the sound of silence howling
On the border between me and my body...
I seek refuge in the isolation of a train
Running indifferently....on the tracks of life
And the wounded memories took shelter in me
An unrelenting darkness was my travel
  companion
And you were not there!

Tehran, 1997

برزخی... دنیا‌یم را به خنده گرفته
هلهله می‌کند
زوزه‌ی زمان و مکان
در نقطه‌ی تلاقی جنون و خرد
دست‌های پوسیده‌ی خاطراتش
آشنایی می‌یابد.
باران‌های فراموشی گه‌گاه می‌بارد
و قصیده‌ی پنهانش را
طوفانِ بی امانِ کلمات
فاش می کند
نگفته‌هایش وحشت‌نامه‌ای است
تک‌تازی‌ست
در کارزارِ دلهره
که رَجزهای تلخش
دلِ دنیا را می‌لرزاند.

شیراز با مادرم در بیمارستان نمازی
شهریور ۱۳۷۶

Being in limbo...has made a mockery of my world
It Ululates
Howls of time and place
At the intersection of insanity and reason
Its decomposing hands of memory
Get acquainted.
The occasional rain of oblivion
And its hidden *qasideh*[8]
Is revealed
By the relentless flood of words.
What goes unsaid is a book of horrors.
A solo rider
In the battlefield of anxiety
With its bitter bragging
Shakes the heart of the world.

Shiraz with my mother at the Namazi Hospital
September 1997

با تازیانه‌ی صداش
کوه می‌هراسد
پناه می‌گیرد
در آغوش باد...
و خیالِ خسته‌ی من
دخیل می‌بندد
بر دست‌های پریشانِ شعر...

تهران، آذر ۷۶

Afraid of the whiplash of its sound
The Mountain
Seeks shelter
In the embrace of the wind...
And my weary imagination
Ties prayer ribbons
To the frenzied hands of poetry...

Tehran, December 1997

سرگردان...
با اندیشه‌ی هزار جهان
وَ سهمی از هیچ........

تهران، ۷۲/۷/۶

Disoriented
With thoughts of a thousand worlds
And no shares in any of them...

Tehran, 28 September 1993

آشوبی است با برگ‌های سپیدار
در رقصِ بی‌قرار باد
دست‌های لرزان بید
دلشوره‌ی درختان
در همهمه‌ی چنار
مویه‌ی نارنجستان
در مرگِ سرو
بادِ بیقرار...!
دردِ سرگردان را
به تساوی توزیع کن
در خاموشی شبانه‌ی ما

تهران، ۱۳۷۴

There is commotion in the poplar leaves
In the restless dance of the wind
The trembling hands of the weeping willow
The anxiety of the trees
In the hubbub of the plane tree
The grief of the sour orange grove
For the death of the cypress
Restless wind...!
Divide the roaming pain
Equally
In our nightly silence

Tehran, 1995

کتیبه‌ای نامفهوم است
زمین
دور مدارِ واهی خود می‌گردد
جای دوری که نَه...
دور دیوانگی خود...
با سماجتی مشکوک

تهران، ۱۳۷۰

It's an undecipherable inscription
The earth
Rotates around its illusory axis
Not a faraway place...
But around its own madness...
With suspicious persistence

Tehran, 1991

تو تنها نرینه‌ای نیستی
که بر گردباد خشم می نشانی‌ام
از تحقیرم آرام...
بر آبگینه‌ام...همچون هیولایی
بختک تو
سخت وُ سنگین
وَ من مادینه‌ای استاده در سکوت...

تهران، ۱۳۷۰/۴/۲۰

44

You're not the only male being
Who sets me on a tornado of anger
Who calms down by insulting me...
In my mirror....like a monster
Your incubus
Heavy and pressing
And I,...a female being, standing in
   complete silence...

Tehran, 11 July 1991

بی‌آن‌که با شما باشم
شمایانم...!
سرگشته...
میانِ زمین وُ آسمانم...

تهران، مهر ۱۳۶۵

46

Without being with you
I am all of you...!
Disoriented...
Between the earth and the sky...!

Tehran, October 1986

شعری سروده‌ام که واژه‌ها از آن گریخته‌اند
ایندرا با هزار چشم می‌گردد
دنبالِ واژه‌هاش...
من شاعری در محاقم

تهران، ۷۶/۶/۳۱

48

I have written a poem from which
   words have escaped
Indra, with a thousand eyes,
is looking for the words....
I am a poet in decline

Tehran, 22 September 1997

FROM THE COLLECTION
EARTH'S CROSSED EYES
(1997–2000)

تاریک می‌شوم
از دفترم که می‌گریزد
ماه......

تهران، ؟

I grow dark
When the moon....
Escapes my notebook

Tehran, n.d.

تا پایان قرن
پاسی از من گذشته است
خوابیده‌ام
میان علف‌های هرز
به چراهای بالا نگاه می‌کنم

تهران، ؟

By the end of the century
Some time will have passed me by
I am lying
In the weeds
Gazing at the "whys" above me

Tehran, n.d

صبح...

خسته.......

خمیازه می‌کشد

جهان پیر می‌شود

در آسمانِ هر روز...

تهران، ؟

Morning....
              weary....
                       Yawns
The world ages
In the everyday sky.

Tehran, n.d.

بهار که بود
به هیأت دوشیزه‌ای معصوم
شیطانی بودم
که به عبادت
خدا را فریفتم
*

بهار که بود
چشمانِ عاشقم
نگرانی مردی را مأمنی شد
پُر غرور
این‌سان فریبش دادم
*

برای تمامی فصل‌ها
به افسون شعر
خدا را نَه...وَ عشق را...
خویشتنم را فریفتم

تهران، ؟

At springtime
In the form of an innocent demoiselle
I was a devil
Who tricked God
Through prayer
*

At springtime
My loving eyes
Sheltered the anxiety of a man
Filled with pride
That's how I tricked him
*

In all seasons
Under the spell of poetry
It was neither God...Nor love...
I tricked myself

Tehran, n.d.

خیالی بی‌افسار
شب تا کلاغ‌های همیشه عزادار
شاعرانی مُرده
وَ هی‌هیِ عریانِ اندیشه
رودِ اندوهی از گورستان...تا نگاه...
ماهِ بی قرار...!
به دنبالم نیا...!
طالع دختران
صبرزار شبی است
که جیغ می‌کشد
و دلتنگی شب را نمی‌شکافد

تهران، تابستان ۷۸

Unbridled imagination
From night to the ever-mourning crows
Dead poets
And the click, click of pure thought
A river of sorrow from the graveyard....to
   the gaze...
Restless moon!
Don't follow me...!
The girls' fate
Is the patience-land of a night
That screams
But does not crack open the night's blues.

Tehran, Summer 1999

زنگِ مرگ را که زد
دستپاچه
روبه‌روی آینه ایستادم
ظلمت بود
فریادِ آینه رانشنیدم

تهران، پاییز ۷۶

As death's bell tolled
Flustered
I stood in front of the mirror
It was dark
I didn't hear the mirror's cry

Tehran, Fall 1997

قارقارِ کلاغی نیمه‌جان
روبه پنجرهی اندوه‌زار...عشق را پراند...
اندوه را نسروده‌ام...
پسرانم در افریقا گرسنه‌اند
حیاتی از اندوه می‌خواهند دخترانم
که آرزوهایشان
در ویرانه‌های هرات می‌گردد...
در هراس...به فراموشی نیاز دارم وُ این دردِ
بی‌چاره
ای کاش عشق پیرهنش را عوض کند

تهران، پاییز ۷۸

The caws of a half-dead crow
Facing the window of sorrow-land...
    made love fly away...
I haven't written the sorrow...
My sons are hungry in Africa
My daughters want a life of sorrow
Whose dreams
Wander in the ruins of Herat...
In fear...I need oblivion and this
    incurable pain
I wish love would change its shirt.

Tehran, Fall 1999

با تن‌پوشی از گمان...سرد بود
اندوه‌زار نم‌نمک خاکستر می‌شد
مَردم مُرده بودند
در خطوط سرگشته‌ی دنیا گم شدم
برهنه‌تراز سکوت
وَ گلوگاهم خسته ازعشق
نق نق بی‌جوابی بودم
بغبغوی مزاحمِ کبوتری پیر
که با سنگ‌واژه‌های پرخاش تلخ‌تر شدم
یادخانه‌ی پوسیده‌ای
و مارستانی در هر سو
اقامت خوشی داشته باشی......زن!

تهران، زمستان ۷۸

In a cloak of doubt...it was cold
The sorrow-land was slowly turning into
   ashes
People had perished
I got lost in the jumbled lines of the world
More naked than silence
And my throat wounded by love
I was an unanswered nag
The disturbing coo of an old pigeon
Growing bitter with harsh aggressive words
A rotten memory-house
A snake pit in every corner
Enjoy your stay....Woman!

Tehran, Winter 2000

کلاغ‌ها که زاییدند
دریای آسمان طوفانی شد
وَ شنبه‌های تقویم...پاره...پاره
از بهار تا دلمرگی
بی‌تابی بود
وَسهمم سرگشتگی
به دنبال چشمی دنیا را گشتم
از پاریایی
در کناره‌ی رود گَنگ
یک چشم خریدم
به بهای یک بوسه نجس

تهران، بهار ۷۷

When the crows gave birth
The sea of the sky became stormy
And the Saturdays on the calendar....torn to
    pieces
From spring to depression
There was restlessness
And my share: confusion
I roamed the earth in search of an eye
And bought an eye
From a pariah
On the banks of Ganges river
for the price of an unclean kiss

Tehran, Spring 1998

خاک کهنه‌ات را
به زخم‌های عشق می‌کشم
تا باورم را گم نکرده باشم
در اندوه‌هزاران پشتِ خانه رهایم کردی
وَ سال‌هاست از من دوری
در رنج‌زار اینجا
چشم که می‌گردد
بوی آشنای سیگارت
در تنهایی خیابان
انتظارم را می‌کشد
سیه‌چرده‌تر از آن روزهایی
تمام حواسم را رنگ گرمسیری‌ات می‌سوزاند
هنوز خیس اندوهی
دستان پینه‌بسته‌ات
مساحتِ مهر را بیدار می‌کند
مردان در سال‌های خستگی
فصل‌ها را فراموش کرده‌اند
از پسِ گردنه‌های مجهول و سال‌های غریب

With your ancient soil
I coat the wounds of love
Not to lose my faith.
You abandoned me in the sorrow-lands
  behind the house
For years, you have been away from me
Here, in the land of suffering.
As I look around
The familiar scent of your cigarette
In the loneliness of the street
Is waiting for me.
Your complexion is darker than those days
Your tropical complexion burns all my senses
Still wet from sorrow
Your calloused hands
Awaken the zone of kindness.
In the weary years, the men
Have forgotten the seasons
Around unknown bends and estranged years

خیالِ دلبستگی‌هایت
از جنوبِ عشقم گذشت
تا بوی اندوه آمدم
و به خیال‌های از یاد رفته پناه بردم...

با خاطره‌ی پدرم
تهران، بهار ۱۳۷۹

The thought of your passions
Passed to the south of my love
I reached the scent of sorrow
And took refuge in forgotten thoughts...

In memory of my father,
Tehran, Spring 2000

به یاد روزی که مجسمه‌ی بودا در غار الورا لبخند زد و
سال‌های اعتکاف در زیر درخت انجیر معابد (پیپال) و
نوای اندوهگین کلاغ‌ها و نور معرفتی که بر درخت تابید
و بر من نَه...

کِی بود
ذهن دنیا در من پیر شد...؟
گَنگ از کناره‌ی من می‌گذشت
در چشم های اریب بودا
باریکه‌ای از جهان
لبخند زد
در تقویم صدای کلاغ می آید...
هزاره‌ی چندم است...؟

*

شب پهن شد...وَ گوشه‌های خانه تلخ...
در تقویم وقتی برای لبخند نیست
بگو...! کدام اندوه را بسرایم...؟ اندوه کدام‌تان را...؟

*

Remembering the days when Buddha's statue in Ellora caves smiled and the years of meditation under the temple's fig tree with the sorrowful song of crows and the light of knowledge that shone on the tree but not on me...

When was it
That the world grew weary in me...?
Ganges river would pass by me,
In the slanted eyes of the Buddha
A slice of the world
Smiled
Crows are heard in the calendar...
Which millennium is it...?

*

Night spread...and the corners of the bitter
    house...
There is no entry in the calendar for smiles
Tell me...! Which sorrow should I write about?
    Which one of your sorrows...?

*

جهان پوسیده است
وَ جیغ کلاغ‌های پوسیده خورشید را تاریک می‌کند
در این هزاره‌ی خسته
بر گلوگاه خسته‌ام
کدام زن...
مرهم خواهد گذاشت...؟

تهران، پاییز ۱۳۷۷

The world is rotten
And the shriek of rotted crows turns the
   sun dark
In this weary millennium
On my wounded throat
Which woman...
is going to apply a salve...?

Tehran, Autumn 1998

نَه اندوه‌زارانِ جنوب

نَه چارراه حیرانی...

برگ‌های تلخ اندیشه

در خستگی فصل‌ها ورق می‌خورد...بی‌حوصله

و امیدهای کپک‌زده...نشخوار می‌شود

به ناگزیر...

تهران، زمستان ۱۳۷۷

Neither those southern valleys of sorrow
Nor the crossroads of confusion...
The bitter leaves of thought
boringly leafed through in the weariness
    of the seasons....
And moldy hopes...are contemplated
Inevitably...

Tehran, Winter 1999

در خطوطِ هراسناک دستانِ لاغرم
دنیا گُم شد...
در چله‌نشینیِ گیج‌ناکی
نشانی لحظه‌هایم...
واژه‌های گمشده بود وُ سکوت...
و گذر از پرسش، دردناک
شاعری سرگشته
در بدایت زمان و نهایت ناگزیرش
جهان را از یاد برد
سرگشته به دنبال مداری موهومم
و دنیا...هنوز ابلهانه می‌دود...

با خیام در تهران، بهار ۱۳۷۸

In the terrifying contours of my thin hands
The world got lost...
In a dizzying forty-day-spiritual-seclusion
The whereabouts of my moments....
Were lost words and silence...
Passing by inquiries, painful
A dazed poet
In the dawn of time and its inevitable finitude
Forgot the world
Dazed, I search for an imaginary orbit
And the world....is still running aimlessly...

With Khayyam in Tehran,
Spring 1999

در رفت و آمد است
سکوت...
وَ ملال...
خیال پیر شدن ندارد

تهران، ۱۳۷۹

Silence....
Is in transit
And Sadness...
Has no intention of aging

Tehran, 2000

به فصل‌ها که می‌زنم دست...

...فرومی ریزند

تجربه می‌کنم به ناگاه...

من...

شکل دیگری از مرگم

.

تهران، پاییز ۱۳۷۹

As I touch the seasons...

...They crumble

I feel, all of a sudden....

I...

Am another embodiment of death

Tehran, Autumn 2000

سراغ از که بگیرم...؟
به ساعتم نگاه کردم
دنیا تمام شد...
وَ ماه می‌گریزد هنوز...
در خالیِ آسمان.

هستی...
بر گردهٔ بی‌تابیِ آهو
هنوز هم...
به ساعتم نگاه کردم
دنیا...
ت...

تهران، تابستان ۱۳۷۶

Whom should I ask...?
I looked at my watch
The world ended...
And the moon is still on the run...
In the emptiness of the sky.
Being
on the deer's restlessness side
Still....
I looked at my watch
The world...
e...

Tehran, Summer 1997

چرا...؟ ماه مُرده‌ای هر روز به خانه‌ام می‌آید

تا وامدار زیستنم کند

مگر در انتهای تمام قصه‌ها جهان نمی‌میرد

وَ من به دار پرسش‌ها آویخته نمی‌شوم...؟

تهران، ؟

Why...? A dead moon comes to my
   home everyday
To make me indebted to life
Doesn't the world die at the end of
   every story
And I end up on the gallows of
   inquiries, hanging?

Tehran, n.d.

با غمخانه‌اش که از جهان وسیع‌تر بود...
همیشه قصه‌های موهوم می‌ساخت
و در انتهایش جهان می‌مُرد
روزی دور با چشمان قدیمی‌اش گُم شد
در آسمانی که فرسوده از راه رسید

با مادرم در تهران، ۱۳۷۹

With her house-of-sorrow, more expansive
    than the world...
She always made up nonsensical tales
Where the world would die in the end
In the distant past, she got lost with her
    ancient eyes
In a sky that arrived, wearily

With my mother in Tehran, 2000

یادِ جوانی‌ام را
از عکس‌ها برمی‌دارم
سوار بر طوفانِ واژه‌ها
به آوارِ خیال می‌روم...
تا جهان در تلخی بی‌قراری‌هایم
پرواز کند
دروازه مرگ بسته بماند
جغرافیای رهایی راه گورستان را گم کند

تهران، ؟

I pick the memory of my youth
from pictures
Riding the flood of words
I go to the ruins of imagination...
So that the world would take flight
In my bitter restlessness
The gate of death would remain shut
The geography of freedom would lose its
    way to the graveyard

Tehran, n.d.

چرا تمام حافظه‌ی دنیا

در لحظه‌هایم می‌گردد

دنبال آه...؟

آوازِ نگران جهان جای دوری نمی‌رود

ببین چگونه چشم‌های لوچ زمین

از هرطرف که می‌رود ویرانی‌است

و من با مرزهای بسته‌ی تنهایی بمبار می‌شوم

تهران، ؟

Why does all the world's memory
in my moments
search for sighs...?
The anxious song of the world doesn't go
very far
See how the crossed eyes of the earth
Whichever way they go, leads to ruins
And I am bombarded by the closed
borders of loneliness

Tehran, n.d.

FROM THE COLLECTION
SILENCE OF THIS SIDE OF JUMBLED LINES
(2001–2016)

سرگشته...
باز می‌گردم...بی توشه‌ای
به اعماق خود رفته بودم

تهران، اردیبهشت ۱۳۸۲

Disoriented
I return...without any provision
I had delved deeply into my soul

Tehran, May 2003

کودکی کهنه‌ام
که برای همیشه گمشده‌ام
در غوغای جهان
دستم پُراز واژه‌های خسته‌ای‌ست
که از دورها آمده‌اند
بر آب می‌نویسم.... دریاها آتش می‌گیرند
گمشده‌ام... در میانه‌ی شب زارها...
وَ سپیدی کاغذ
مکانِ امنی نیست
رازِ این سکوت
وُ همه‌ی این سال‌ها...!

تهران، ؟

I am a worn out child
Forever lost
In the world's turmoil
My hands are full of stale words
from far away
I write on water...seas catch fire
I am lost...
in the midst of nightscapes
And the whiteness of paper
Is no safe haven
The mystery of this silence
And all these years...!

Tehran, n.d.

در آشپزخانه گُم که می‌شوم
دنیا هم چشم بگذارد
پیدایم نمی‌کند ماه...

تهران، ۱۳۸۴

When I get lost in the kitchen
Even if the world closes its eyes
I won't be found by the moon...

Tehran, 2005

تمام سال‌های دلهره
از دیروزها می‌گذرد
فردا...
خیالی بی قرار است
طعم تلخی دارد
کنار آمدن با این روزها...

تهران، ؟

All the years of anxiety
Pass through yesterdays.
Tomorrow...
Is a restless thought.
Coming to terms with these days...
Has a bitter taste...

Tehran, n.d,

به دار پرسش بودم
به روزهای جهان
به هراسِ باریکی از مرگ
به تکه‌ای از شب...

تهران، ۱۳۸۱

I hung
On the gallows of inquiry
On days of life
On a narrow fear of death
On a piece of the night...

Tehran, 2002

فصل‌های رفته...
کلاغی پوسیده وُ قارقاری یاوه بود
بر گندزاری   بی پنجره...بی پرسش.
فصل های نیامده....
کفتاری است که لیس می‌زند
زخم‌های دلم را...

تهران، مهر ۱۳۸۲

Bygone seasons...
Were rotten crows and nonsensical caws
In a swamp—no windows...no inquiries
Forthcoming seasons...
A vulture who licks
The wounds of my heart...

Tehran, October 2003

به کوه می‌خورَد رؤیایم
سنگ می‌شود...
وَ چون کلاغی   بی‌گاه
دست‌های آسمان را رو می‌کند

تهران، ؟

My dream runs into the mountain
It turns to stone...
And like a crow—untimely
Tips the sky's hand

Tehran. n.d.

با واژه‌هایم درهم می‌ریزد جهان

فردا واژه‌ای رهاست...بی طبق‌های نذری وُ نوحه

از چین‌های پنجه کلاغی‌ام سال‌ها می‌گذرد...

نیامده بودی که برنگردی...! مثل تیمارستان‌های

روز به انفرادی

پریشانی‌ام را زنجیر می‌کنی

جهانگرد سلولم به سکوت می‌رسد

زبان آویخته

بر گذرگاه جهنم

زنم...

تهران، ۱۳۸۸

With my words, the world turns upside down
Tomorrow is an unfettered word....without
   trays of donated food and religious chants
Years pass through the folds of my crabgrass....
You didn't come to not return..!
Like psych wards, these days you chain my
   distress to a solitary cell
The world traveler of my cell falls silent
With my tongue hanging out
On the path to hell
I am a woman...

Tehran, 2009

در خانه بی‌دریغ صرف می‌شوم

در فعل‌های ناگزیر...

میانِ کوچه‌ی عادت

خانه‌ی شماره‌ی دیروز

برزخی که پشت پنجره روییده

و شب‌های این‌همه آبستن...

تهران، ۱۳۸۷

At home, I am totally consumed
By mandatory chores...
In the midst of the alley of habits
In the house numbered yesterday
In the uncertainty spread outside the window
And nights so heavily pregnant....

Tehran, 2008

در آه...

غرق شده‌ام...

وَ کاش.... را در آسمان هنوز دنبال می‌کنم

که به مقصد نمی‌رسد

دودِ سکوت

بر روزهای پریشان سُر می‌خورد

وَ مرگ...

پناهِ ایمنی می‌شود

با دو دست گشاده‌اش   بر سنگفرشِ امروز

امروز معجزه قمری یاکریمی است که پشتِ پنجره‌ی

تشویش اهلی شده

و قلب خیال‌های ما را نشانه گرفته...

تهران، ۱۳۸۸

116

I have drowned...
In a sigh...
And I follow "I wish"... in the sky of yet
As it fails to reach its destination.
The fumes of silence
Glide on chaotic days
And death...
Becomes a safe haven
With its arms open—on pavements of today
Today is the miracle of a collared dove,
   domesticated outside the window of
   anxiety
Targeting the depths of our imagination....

Tehran, 2009

گاهی که در روزگار نمی‌گنجم

وَ حوصله‌ی فصل‌ها سَر می‌رود

به کبوترِ خِنگی دلخوشم

که مدام دور خودش می‌گردد وَ بغبغو می‌کند

در ایوانِ خانه

تلویزیون روی ویرانه‌ی تنم جنگ می‌کند

روزنامه سیاست...

سکوت وُ بغض وُ دلهره اتاق‌های دلم را اشغال کرده‌اند

تهران، ۱۳۸۸

Sometimes when I feel out of place
And the seasons lose patience
I take pleasure in a witless pigeon
That runs in circles, cooing
On the balcony of the house
The TV fights a war on the ruins of
    my body
The newspaper tortures me...
Silence and anxiety and tears have
    occupied the chambers of my heart.

Tehran, 2009

گاهی که خودم را می‌نویسم
کلاغی گمشده‌ام
در ازدحام خیابان‌های شلوغ شهر

*

آن‌گاه که فکر می‌کنی دوستت دارم
آرزوهایم را تبعید کرده‌ام
وَ به آینه‌ای که مرا نمی‌شناسد گریخته‌ام

*

اکنون به پاره آرزویی آویخته‌ام
تا جهان را بگویم
با قارقارِ تلخم
هر چند صله‌ام   سنگپاره‌ای...

تهران، ۱۳۸۸

Sometimes, as I write my self
I am a lost crow
In the congestion of crowded city streets
*

The moment you think I love you
I have exiled my hopes
And escaped to a mirror that doesn't
    recognize me
*

I have clung to a piece of hope
To tell the world
With my harsh caw caws
Though the reward for my poetry
    is—a cobblestone...

                                    Tehran, 2009

تیمارستانی که با من است
همیشه تنهاست
وَ جای خالی تمامِ دیوانگان
سکوت کرده است
مرگ با قبای سیاهش در می زند
تیمارستان به موهای ژولیده‌اش دست
می‌کشد
وَ به کلاغی لال فکر می‌کند
که آوازهایش را کجا خواهد خواند...؟

تهران، ۱۳۸۹

The mental institution that is with me
Is always lonely
And the empty space of all the mental
    patients
Has fallen silent.
Death with its black robe knocks
The mental institution touches its
    uncombed hair
And thinks about a mute crow
Wondering where it would sing its songs…?

Tehran, 2010

به اتاق تمام مُردگان جهان سر می‌کشم
کتاب‌ها را می‌کاوم
و نشانی نمی‌یابم
به جست جوی گمشده‌ای
که نمی‌دانم چیست؟ کجاست؟ کیست؟
همه را خوانده‌ام...جز یک شعر!

تهران، ۱۳۹۰

I peek in the rooms of all the dead in the world
I dig through books
And I find no clue
In search of a lost one
without knowing what, where or who it is?
I have read it all...except a poem!

Tehran, 2011

همه‌ی پسین‌های اندوهناک
در من غروب کرده‌اند
گمشده در خویش
شامگاهی تلخم
که به سکوت می‌روم
وَبامدادی که از ترس در تن‌پوشی سیاه گُم شده است.

تهران، دی ۱۳۸۲

All these sorrowful dusks
Have sun-setted in me.
Lost in myself
I am a harsh twilight
That falls silent
And a fearful dawn lost in a black cloak.

Tehran, January 2004

جنون که می‌وزد
کلمات هم درمانم نمی‌کند
آرام به خاطرم می‌آیی
بی‌خبر در فصل‌ها گم می‌شوی.....

تهران، ۱۳۸۲

When madness blows
Not even words can cure me
Gently you come to my mind
Without notice, you get lost in the seasons.....

Tehran, 2014

آموخته‌ام
رؤیایم را
آرام آرام بگریم
وَ عشق را
در تازشِ تندبادها
در کاغذی سفید حبس کنم
و با اتاقی که جز خیال، پنجره‌ای ندارد
زن باشم

تهران، ۱۳۹۱

I have learned
To shed my dream softly
And to imprison
Love
In the midst of hurricanes
On a white sheet of paper
And to be a woman
With a room whose only window is
   imagination

Tehran, 2013

مِه

فرو می‌ریزد

سرگشتگی‌اش را

وَتو بر مانیتور کوچکم

زیبایی دست نیافتنی‌ات را

وَمن نمی‌دانم با آن همه زیبایی چه کنم...؟

دستم به خنده‌هایت نمی‌رسد

مِه شده‌ای

وَ از لابه‌لای خیالم می‌گذری

بوی زیبایی‌ات را در آسمانم دنبال می‌کنم

همچون سال‌های سر به هوایی که بی‌پروا

فرو می‌رفتم   در آسمانی خالی

تهران، ۲۰ آذر ۱۳۹۲

The fog

Dissipates

Its confusion

And you on my small monitor

Dissipate your unattainable beauty

And I don't know what to do with all this
   beauty...?

I can't reach your laughter

You have turned into fog

And you pass through the crevices of my
   mind

I follow the scent of your beauty in my sky

Like the giddy years when carelessly

I'd sink—in a vast sky

Tehran, 11 December 2013

جهان از کنارم می‌گذرد   شتابان

بهره‌ایم نیست

جز شعرهایی که در آغوشم بغض کرده‌اند

دهن‌بندی که مردان به تکریم هدیه‌ام دادند

چشم‌بندی که مهریه‌ام بود

و دُشواژه‌هایی بی‌دریغ......

پیش از آن‌که خودسر شوم

از سفیدی کاغذهای مچاله

رمز فریادهایم را برگیر

تهران، ۱۳۹۱

The world passes me by—hastily
I have nothing to gain
Except the poems on the verge of tears in
   my embrace
The muzzle honorifically bestowed upon
   me by men
The blindfold that was my alimony
And copious insults...
Before I become obstinate
Decipher the secrets of my outcries
From the whiteness of crumpled papers.

Tehran, 2012

سپیدهدم...تهنشین کرده   هوای خاکستریاش را
در چشمان تو........
جزیرهی مجنون تنهاست...
از دشتِ لیلی   عابری نمیگذرد
دزدانه با دلم میگویم
ازچشمان توهم...!

تهران، ۲ دی ۱۳۹۲

Dusk...has settled its gray air
In your eyes...
The Island of Majnun is lonely...
No one passes by in Layli's field
Sneakily I tell my heart
Even from your eyes...!

Tehran, 23 December 2013

ارتباط من و تو

همین کلمات بازیگوشی است

که ناخودآگاه از مداد سیاهم می‌پرند

وَ در سرمای بی‌درجه‌ی این روزها...

نقشه‌های ذهنی‌ات را خط‌خطی می‌کنند

تهران، ۲۶ آذر ۱۳۹۲

The connection between you and me
Are these playful words
That unconsciously spring from my
    black pencil
And in the frigid cold of these days...
Scribble over your mental atlas.

Tehran, 17 December 2013

از الفبای زبانم تنها   آه...را به یاد می‌آورم
وراهِ کشتزار خشخاشی
که به نگاه تو می‌رسد...

تهران، ۱۳۹۳

From the alphabet of my language—I only
   remember the ah....
And the way to the bitter poppy field
That reaches your gaze...

                                   Tehran, 2014

مترسک سیاهی شدم

شبی با شعرهایی تلخ...

زاغی بور مرا به یاد می‌آورد

که در جمعه‌های انقراض پرپر می‌زند

فریاد برنیامده‌ای‌ست...بغض فروخورده‌ام

در آغوشِ این‌همه دیوار وُ شبانان دوُروُبَر...

وَ سکوتم...پرچمِ بی‌قراری است که به هیچ

سوگندی تن در نمی دهد

تهران، ۱۳۹۴/۷/۱۲

I turned into a black scarecrow
One night with bitter poems...
A ground jay fluttering in the Fridays of
  extinction
will remember me
It's an unreleased cry...a swallowed lump
  in my throat
Embraced by all these walls and the
  shepherds all around...
And my silence...is a restless flag that does
  not surrender to any pledge.

Tehran, 4 October 2015

سکوت این سوی خط‌های درهم
دیوانه‌ای است که به هیچ شاعری شباهت ندارد
واژه‌های گریخته...سطرهای دربه‌در
آینده‌ای بی‌کلام...
دیوانگی شاخ‌هایش را در شعرم جا گذاشته...

تهران، ۱۳۹۵

The silence on this side of the jumbled lines
Is a lunatic who resembles no poet
Escaped words...vagabond lines
A wordless future...
Madness has left its horns in my poem...

Tehran, 2016

اگر شعر نبود

که صخره‌های رؤیا را وطنم کند

درد را کلمه به کلمه در دهان دوست داشتن بگذارم

دنیا...تبعیدگاه دلتنگی بود

اگر شعر نبود

جنون و کلمه و کشتزار خشخاش

به من دل نمی‌بستند

If poetry did not exist[9]
To turn the cliffs of my dreams into my
    homeland
To place pain word by word in the mouth
    of love
The world... would be nostalgia's exile
If poetry did not exist
Insanity and words and
bitter poppy fields
Would not become attached to me

گره به اندوهی...
به داری...
به دردی...
به شب‌های ناوقت ...
به کابوس‌های کهنه...
به دلهره...که همراه ما در پیاده‌روها قدم می‌زند
تا نیمه‌های مرگ...
نگران اندوه ما نیست...دنیا

Tied to a heartache[10]

To a gallows

To a pain

To untimely nights

To old nightmares

To anxiety

That walks beside us on the sidewalk

Until half-dead

Is unconcerned about our sorrow...the world

PREVIOUSLY UNPUBLISHED POEMS SENT
BY THE POET TO THE TRANSLATOR

خاطراتی که به سفر می‌روند
هرگز باز نمی‌گردند
نیمی در مِه
خانه را گم می‌کنند

Traveling memories
Never return
Half-covered in fog
They lose their way home

کلمه‌ای محو شده در دستنویسی پاره پاره ام
اشتیاقی نَه به خوانده شدن
نَه گم شدن در تو

I am a faded word on a torn up manuscript
No desire to be read
Nor to get lost in you

کلماتی به کاغذ نرسیده‌ام
در خیال
پرپر می‌شوم

I am words not yet landed on paper
In my mind
I come undone

کابوسی است

زندگی

به انتظارِ خوابی دراز

It's a nightmare
Life
awaiting a long slumber

از ارتفاع کدام کابوس افتاده‌اند؟
کلماتی که به کاغذ نرسیده
پرپر می‌شوند
وَ این مدادِ نیمه نصفه
هم‌چون پرنده‌ای بی‌قرار
درمیانِ انگشتانم پرپر می‌زند

From the heights of which nightmare have
   they fallen?
Words which before reaching the paper
Shed their petals
And this half-used pencil
Like a restless bird
Frantic between my fingers

به خانهٔ تلخی می‌مانم
با اضلاعی حواس پرت
در میدانِ تنهایی
پنجره‌ی رو به شرقم اضطراب را بیدار می کند
اندوه، پنجره غربم را سرگشته تر
هیچ اتفاقی از خنده
به من دورتر نیست

I resemble a bitter house
With distracted dimensions
In loneliness square
My east-facing window awakens anxiety
Sorrow renders my west-facing window
    more perplexed
No event is further from me than laughter

دلتنگیم پنجره را باز...
خیال، آغوشم را...
تو نیستی
وَ زخم‌هایم بغض کرده اند
ادامه‌ی اندوهی بن‌بستم
که هر روز عمیق‌تر می‌شوم

My blues open a window...
Hope opens my embrace...
You're not here
My wounds are on the verge of tears
I'm the continuation of the dead-end
   of sorrow
Deepening further each day

اندازه‌ی مرگ شده‌ام
وَ می‌توانم از شاخه‌ی بلندترین سپیدار
تاریکی را لمس کنم
چقدر اندوه دور دنیا بپیچد
در دنیای من ته نشین شود
که جمعه‌ها را زنجیر کنم؟
وارونه‌ام و سقف این خانه عجیب دلگیر
است
هر صبح که پیر می‌شود
رَدِّ پای دلتنگی
از سفیدی کاغذ
چک...
چک ...
چکه می کند
وَ در تنهاییم پنهان می شود

I have grown as big as death
And I can feel the darkness
from the branches of the tallest poplar
How much sorrow should swirl around
  the world
Before it settles in my world
So that I can shackle Fridays?
I am upside down and the ceilings in this
  house are awfully depressing
As it ages each morning
The footprints of depression
Drip...
        Drip...
                Drips from
The whiteness of the paper
And hides in my loneliness

نپرس چرا تلخم

وَ قار قار کلاغها

مرا کنار تو می‌نشاند..؟

نپرس چرا اخم‌هایم شبیه دشنام است

و پیچ و تاب‌های مشکوک

ارتفاع گمان را

به سرگیجه‌ی تردید می‌زند

تا تمامِ طوطی‌های دوروبرم را فراری دهد

تردید بادِ هوا نیست

که در سلولِ هر کسی جا خوش کند

میزبان بیقراری می‌خواهد

وُ شاعری خودسر

که تمام کاغذهای دنیا را از درد تاریک کند

در فصل‌هایی‌که مشغولیت مردن است

آسمانِ پوسیده هم که شرمسارِ کسی نیست

بیا... این زوزه‌های ظلمت را ورق بزنیم

وَ این گرگهای سر به هوا را

که سهمِ عشقِ مرا شلاق می‌زنند

Don't ask why I'm bitter
And the crows caw caws
Seat me next to you...?
Don't ask why my frown is like an insult
And it collides
the suspicious curves
At the height of doubt
With the vertigo of disbelief.
To make all the parrots around me take flight
Doubt is not like the wind
That takes refuge in just anyone's cells
It needs a restless host
And a stubborn poet
To darken all the paper in the world with pain
In seasons preoccupied with death.
The rotten sky is not ashamed of anyone either
Let's leaf through these howls of darkness
And these distracted wolves
That flog my share of love.

Notes

1. پوران فرخزاد.۱۳۷۶ اوهام سرخ شقایق. برگزینی از اشعار زنان زمان. تهران: انتشارات ناژین، صفحه‌ی ۳۷۸

2. It appeared in Pouran Farrokhzād's *Ohām-e Sorkh-e Shaqāyeq* (Poppy's red delusions), Tehran: Nazheen, 1998.

3. Ghazal: A poem of between 5-12 couplets where the first hemistich of the first verse rhymes with the second hemistich of all other verses.

4. A long poem where each verse has its own rhyme. This form is well suited for storytelling.

5. Two of the seven poems are included in this translated collection.

6. Poet's footnote: reference to Greek mythology, [specifically Atlas].

7. Poet's footnote: refers to an Arab (Saudi) custom where the tail of a cow would be set on fire. The cow would then cry and the people would pray for rain to save the cow.

8. A poem of fifteen to eighty couplets where the first hemestich of the first verse rhymes with

the second hemistich of all other verses. It is sometimes translated as ode in English.

9. Has previously appeared in *Song of the Ground Jay*, Expanded Edition (Gordyeh Publishers, 2023).

10. Ibid

References

Karachi, Rouhangiz. *Gozineh-ye Ash'ar* [Selected Poems], Tehran: Morvarid Publishers: 2018, pages 22, 24, 29, 32-40, 43-45, 47-48, 50,55, 58, 61-63, 65, 71-74, 77-78, 80, 82-84, 89-93, 95, 99-100, 102, 104-106,115-119, 123-124, 126, 128-130, 139-142, 146, 149, and 160.

This selection includes 11 poems that were provided by the poet. Three of the poems have been previously translated in *Song of the Ground Jay*, Expanded Edition (Gordyeh Publishers, 2023).

Acknowledgements

I am grateful to Dr. Rouhangiz Karachi and her scholarly work which makes room for women poets in Persian literary history. I am also grateful to her for helping in the selection of the poems and sending me some of her unpublished poems to choose from for this bilingual edition.

I am indebted to Dick Davis for taking the time to read the translations. I am honored and humbled by his generosity and kindness.

I am grateful to Mohammad and Najmieh Batmanglij's feedback and support. I am grateful to my daughter Tina who is my most loving and thoughtful sounding board. I am thankful to my partner, Arjang, who lovingly welcomes all my projects, no matter how insane!

I am blessed to have my brother Reza in my life. He is a gentle soul who at once appreciates classical Persian poetry and celebrates the modern verse. His respect for tradition alongside the quest for new knowledge have served as my guiding light.

Other Mage Poetry Titles

Song of the Ground Jay: Poems by Iranian Women, 1960–2022
Bilingual Edition / Selected and Translated by Mojdeh Bahar

Milkvetch and Violets
Mohammad Reza Shafi'i Kadkani / Translated by Mojdeh Bahar

Faces of Love: Hafez and the Poets of Shiraz
Bilingual Edition / Translated by Dick Davis

The Mirror of My Heart:
A Thousand Years of Persian Poetry by Women
Bilingual Edition / Translated by Dick Davis

Vis and Ramin
Fakhraddin Gorgani / Translated by Dick Davis

Khosrow and Shirin
Nezami Ganjavi / Translated by Dick Davis

Layli and Majnun
Nezami Ganjavi / Translated by Dick Davis

Shahnameh: The Persian Book of Kings
Abolqasem Ferdowsi / Translated by Dick Davis

Borrowed Ware: Medieval Persian Epigrams
Introduced and Translated by Dick Davis

When They Broke Down the Door: Poems
Fatemeh Shams / Introduction and translations by Dick Davis

Another Birth and Other Poems
By Forugh Farrokhzad, translated by Hasan Javadi
and Susan Sallée / Bilingual edition

Obeyd-e Zakani: Ethics of Aristocrats and other Satirical Works
translated by Hasan Javadi

Audio Books

Shahnameh: The Persian Book of Kings
Abolqasem Ferdowsi / Translated by Dick Davis
Penguin / Echo Point Audio / Read by
Dick Davis, Sean Rohani, Nikki Massoud

Faces of Love: Hafez and the Poets of Shiraz
Translated by Dick Davis / Penguin Audio / Read by
Dick Davis, Tala Ashe and Ramiz Monsef

The Mirror of My Heart:
A Thousand Years of Persian Poetry by Women
Translated by Dick Davis / Penguin Audio / Read by
Dick Davis, Mozhan Marno, Tala Ashe and Serena Manteghi

Layli and Majnun
Nezami Ganjavi / Translated by Dick Davis
Penguin Audio / Read by
Dick Davis, Peter Ganim, Serena Manteghi and Sean Rohani

Vis and Ramin
Fakhraddin Gorgani / Translated by Dick Davis
Mage Audio / Read by
Mary Sarah Agliotta, Dick Davis (introduction)

My Uncle Napoleon
Iraj Pezeshkzad / Translated by Dick Davis
Mage Audio / Read by
Moti Margolin, Dick Davis (introduction)

Savushun: A Novel about Modern Iran
Simin Daneshvar / Translated by M.R. Ghanoonparvar
Mage Audio / Read by
Mary Sarah Agliotta, Brian Spooner (introduction)

Crowning Anguish: Taj al-Saltana
Memoirs of a Persian Princess
from the Harem to Modernity, 1884–1914
Introduction by Abbas Amanat / Translated by Anna Vanzan
Mage Audio / Read by Kathreen Khavari

www.ingramcontent.com/pod-product-compliance
Lightning Source LLC
Chambersburg PA
CBHW021149160426
42812CB00078B/279